The Roadmap From Learning Disabilities to Success

A step-by-step guide for Parents and Educators to treat the symptoms of Learning Disabilities, ADD/ADHD, Dyslexia, Dyscalculia, Dysgraphia, and more!

Kathy Johnson
2010

Cover design by Leslie Warner¬Rafaniello

www.PyramidOfPotential.com
P.O. Box 103, Burnt Hills, NY 12027
(518) 585-2007

ISBN 978¬0¬9819805¬7¬7

This book follows the story several children who struggled in school, but found success after following the steps outlined in this book: mind and body health, neurodevelopment, sensory-motor development, cognitive development, and academic intervention. Each chapter includes stories, a quiz to see if the chapter is relevant, general information, and resources – do it yourself, on¬line, and professionals.

Praise for
The Roadmap from Learning Disabilities to Success

"Wow! I am truly impressed by the author's commitment to her students to find a road that would help them triumph over learning disabilities. When schools offered modifications without helping the underlying disability, Kathy engaged in an exhaustive research project to find appropriate therapies to help her students. If your child or student is facing an academic roadblock, The Roadmap from Learning Disabilities to Success is a wonderful tool for exploring possibilities you probably have not even considered. Good luck with your journey, Kathy has provided a wonderful guide."-*Elizabeth Meehan, special educator for 25 years*

"Nothing can be more frustrating to a parent than a child who can't read or learn. Unfortunately, parents often find themselves alone as their children continue to struggle despite educational intervention. The Roadmap to Success is an important guide for any parent that has a child with a learning problem. Mrs. Johnson provides us with an invaluable collection of information and resources that provides solutions rather than labels." -*Dr. Robert Fox, OD*

"This book offers a wonderful introduction to the underlying developmental components of learning. Each chapter takes the reader through a journey of discovery of this multifaceted process and offers many valuable resources to help parents, therapists and educators move forward." -*Pamela Formosa, MA OTR/L, Author of FRAID NOT! Empowering Kids with Learning Differences*

"I couldn't put this book down. No one writes about the power of potential with more feeling, understanding, and accuracy as Kathy does. This was a book I could ask my husband to read and know he would read beyond the first few pages because it is straight to the point. I was able to easily pin point what areas I need to work on with my child. I was able to go into my Dr. with confidence that I know what areas my child need help with. I was so empowered; what a great feeling it is as a Mom. Nobody knows a child better than his parents. Most important, Kathy shares her wisdom of how we can help our child in a very healthy way." - *Lynn Kirsch, mom of LD child*

This book is dedicated to Julia.
Thank you my child!

Table of Contents

Table of Contents

Acknowledgements

Thank you to all the people who made this book possible. First and foremost is to my husband Gary, and my children, Julia, Bobby, and Chris. I learned so much from you all! Also, I need to thank the professionals who have taught me to create the Roadmap and Pyramid of Potential: Rob Fox, Judy Hamm, Sam Berne, Steven Larsen, and Rich Herbold. Thank you to Leslie Rafaniello for the cover, to Lauren Marr for editing, and to Elizabeth Meehan, Lynn Kirsch, Rob Fox and Pam Formosa for their kind remarks. Thank you to all the parents who have entrusted me with their children over the years, and thank you, thank you, thank you children for teaching me how to teach you.

Chapter 1: Introduction

In 1996, I was poised to begin my new career in education, after years of being in the business of working with computers and their relationships with the people who use them. I had trained adults for years in classes ranging from beginning word processing, to advanced spreadsheet and database creation. I left that behind when I finished my Masters in Education, specializing in Curriculum Development and Instructional Technology. I had three small children at home who were starting school, a husband who could pay the bills, and a desire to make a true difference in the world. Yes, I was poised and ready to tutor reading!

"I hate myself."
"I hate school."
"I want to kill myself."

These were the words that prompted me to begin my career. They were spoken by children ranging from 9 to 15, who were very intelligent, yet struggled to keep up with their peers in school. These kids did not know they were smart. All they could see was that no matter how hard they tried, they could not do the things their friends could – read, write, do math, and remember spelling words. They thought they were "stupid" when actually, they were learning disabled. They were talented also: excellent in art, music, and sports. However, being at the top in the extracurricular activities did not help their self-esteem enough. School, after all, was 6 hours of torture for them, concentrated on the very areas in which they failed. There was no escape, because the law demanded that they attend. There was no way out.

So, while I thought my new career was teaching reading, actually, it was saving lives.

When deciding exactly what program to use, that would be the most effective, I had a decision to make: what program could I offer that was different than the ones the schools were using. This was important, because the schools were already using the best that they knew in school, then I must choose something different than the school in order to help the struggling reader. I had considered Lindamood-Bell, a program out of California.

There was a training in Washington, DC that I could have attended, but then a reading specialist from Texas, the sister of my friend (also a special education teacher), recommended that I buy a copy of <u>Reading Reflex,</u> by Carmen McGuinness. She had great success with her students, and it was a very cost effective place to start. I order my copy for $32, read it over the weekend once it came, and started my first student the next Monday.

I worked with an 11 year old girl, Jennifer (not her real name; all names have been changed in the book), who was in 4th grade, but had difficulty reading and spelling. After just 20 hours of one-on-one instruction, her reading scores tested above grade level. I was sure this was the silver bullet! I continued to teach using this method, and received certification from Read America with their Phonographix Method, the method from Reading Reflex. Most students did very well.

However, one boy, Jeremy, could read well from Children's Classics in which the lines of text are well spaced and there is a picture on every other page. Once I put him into a grade-level book, <u>Hatchet,</u> he would miss simple words like "bear". I had taught him to read, but not succeed. There was a block.

Jennifer could read, but could she did not have a good memory, causing her problems in reading comprehension, spelling, math, and writing. Being the perfectionist that I am, I needed to know more about how to help these children and others like them so that they could succeed in school and in life.

That began my journey to create the Roadmap to Success, one meandering road at a time, finding dead ends (they are not included in this book), and sometimes finding highways (they are the best of the best, and in each chapter).

However, the map is not complete. It does not include roads that are under construction, or roads that I have not traveled. There are programs, trainings, and therapies that I have yet to discover that work well. I have included in the upcoming chapters those I have found that are effective in helping people of all ages succeed. I wish each of you success in your own journey to success!

How to use the Roadmap

As I helped many people over the last 14 years find the root causes of their struggles and the steps to their success, I developed the Pyramid of Potential.

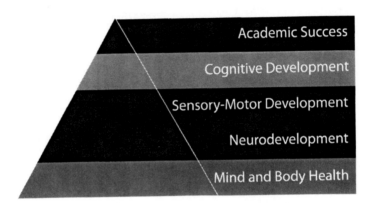

The Pyramid represents the order and importance of the steps that you and your child, student, or client will take on your own journey. The chapters correspond to the various levels of the pyramid.

Sit back and enjoy the ride, and learn how you, too, can make a difference in a child's life.

Chapter 2: Nutrition

Success Story

Martha and her mom were referred to me from Dr. Fox, a behavioral optometrist who noticed that she was not progressing as well as she should in vision therapy. Since he knew that she had auditory processing problems, I would be able to help in that area. In her screening, I noticed that she also had neurodevelopmental delays, so I started her working on inhibiting the Moro Reflex (more on that in chapter 4).

Although she did well with Listening Therapy, she was not progressing well with the reflex inhibition program, so I suggested she see a nutritionist. Once they found ways to include fats into Martha's very limited diet, she was able to move forward, eventually inhibited 3 reflexes, completed vision therapy, and improving her memory to the point that she could remember what she was learning in 6th grade for the first time in her life.

Quiz

Diet:
- Is your child a picky eater?
- Does your child have irregular bowel movements?
- If he/she has not eaten in several hours, is the behavior different?
- Does he/she get hyperactive after eating sugary foods?
- Has your child's diet contained lots of trans fats – found in cookies, pastries, and Crisco?
- Behavior: Food is the ultimate brain chemical!
- Is your child obstinate or defiant – "my way or the highway"?
- Is your child depressed?
- Is your child anxious?
- Does your child have problems paying attention?

If you answered yes to many of these questions, then improved nutrition will likely help the symptoms.
'

General Information

At the base of the Pyramid of Potential is body and mind health. Central to body health is good nutrition. The stuff we put in our bodies is what feeds every cell of our body, including our brains. Let's look at a few processes that contribute to good brain function.

First, let's look at blood sugar. When blood sugar is too low, we cannot think very well. This decrease in brain function can happen if we have not eaten in several hours. We feel scatter-brained and unfocussed. I have found personally that I am much better at making dinner if I eat before I start cooking! Otherwise I find myself looking in the refrigerator many times before being able to make a decision about what food to eat. If blood sugar is too high, from eating foods with a high glycemic index (sugar, white potatoes, white bread, pasta, or pastries), we may have high energy for a while but then crash from low blood sugar. A source of protein eaten at every meal will help reduce the peaks and valleys. Another consideration is the possibility of food intolerances and allergies. Intolerances may look like allergies but not give a positive result to an allergy test. A common intolerance is to milk and lactose, giving the person diarrhea or stomach aches. An intolerance to gluten (primarily wheat and corn) can be in the form of celiac disease.

Learning disabilities, ADHD, and developmental delays are more than doubled in persons with celiac disease.

There are two types of food allergies to consider. The IgE allergy causes hives and other severe immediate reactions, like anaphylactic shock, that you may have heard of, to peanuts, for example. The IgG allergy is more allusive, and reactions happen at least 24 hours after the food is eaten. Therefore it is much more difficult to see a direct relationship between a certain food and the reaction resulting from that food. Reactions may be attention difficulties and/or mood disturbances, as well as digestive issues causing poor absorption. Since our brains consist of cells fed by the food we eat, if there is a digestion issue, there may very well be a cognitive issue as a result.

A third food issue is that of neurotransmitters. Dopamine and Seratonin, the feel-good chemicals in our brains, are made from a combination of amino acids and B vitamins in a very delicate and complex process. When a child has poor digestion, it seems that he/she requires a very large amount of vitamin B complex (as opposed to RDA), in combination with the specific amino acid in order to have a more stable mood, less depression, and a more alert mind.

Why are fats so important? After all, we are taught to eat a low-fat diet, yet for Martha, fat was one of the keys to her success. The brain consists of mostly fat and water and is a complicated electrical machine in which glucose is the fuel.

The brain has trillions of neurons, which are connected to each other with synapses. Any time you learn something new, a new synapse is formed. Repetition of that learning creates a stronger connection. Finally, permanent learning occurs when myelination occurs – when a fatty layer covers the synapse. This is similar to covering bare electrical wires with black electrical tape so that the connection is secure and does not short circuit. Fat in the diet is necessary for the myelination.

The worst fat for the body and brain is trans fats, also called partially hydrogenated oils. These have been chemically modified to create an elongated molecule that may cause poor myelenation in certain people. I suggest that you eliminate them from the diet completely. When reading labels on processed foods, you may see "0 trans fats" advertised on the front of the box, yet you might also see "partially hydrogenated cottonseed oil" as an ingredient. The food manufacturer is allowed to advertise this way because there is less than 1 gram of trans fats in the food. Avoid these as well.

Add in supplements containing fish oils if possible. Add into the diet whole foods that contain fats that are good for the brain: salmon, olive oil, flax seeds, walnuts, almonds, and avocados.

Resources

Do It Yourself

There are a few simple rules to follow to keep your child's blood sugar steady:
• Eat every 3 hours or less.
• Eat protein with every meal.
• Do not overdo the sugar, white potatoes, and baked goods at any meal.

The easiest way to determine if an allergy or intolerance exists is to follow an elimination diet. For two weeks, eliminate the food or foods that may be causing the behavior. Then slowly add in one food at a time. Add in one food for 3 days. If a reaction occurs, immediately eliminate it again. You can try to add it in again two weeks later to be sure it was the food. If that food was OK, add in another. Do not add in two at a time or add another in before 3 days have gone by symptom-free. This is basically a scientific experiment!

Another thing to try is digestive enzymes, purchased at the grocery store or drug store. They help the body digest no matter what the issue, so look for a change in behavior after taking digestive enzymes. There are several from which to choose. Look for one that includes many different enzymes to help digest many types of food.

An excellent book that I have recommended is <u>The UltraMind Solution</u> by Dr. Mark Hyman. This book covers both diet and the neurotransmitters.

Online:

• Dr. Mercola: articles.mercola.com

• Dr. Mark Hyman: ultrawellness.com

Professionals:

To search for a nutritionist in your area go to Findanutritionist.com

Chapter 3: Body and Mind Health: Stress Relief

Success Story

Stress has been found to create such a negative impact on our bodies and brains, that it can create disease. A child, who normally is a high achiever, will do poorly on the day that the dog died, the grandmother is sick, or the parents are fighting. That child's brain is overwhelmed with the important problems of the day, and stress is keeping him / her from learning. Can you imagine how difficult learning must be for the child who has to get on the bus everyday knowing they have to face their teacher and other kids, knowing that they cannot read or do math and knowing that there is no escape?

Jessica had finished the neurodevelopment training, sensory integration, and cognitive training, yet still had some anxiety, so the family searched for some help. They found it with Dr. Larsen, a psychologist who used neuro-biofeedback called LENS. After several months of these treatments, Jessica said that she was able to let people touch her for the first time, and that she was calmer and slept better. Because of the reduction of stress, she was able to attend college away from home.

Quiz

To find out if your child has too much stress, answer the following questions (from the Mayo Clinic web site: http://www.mayoclinic.com/health/stress-symptoms)

Does your child complain of:

- Headache
- Back pain
- Chest pain
- Heart palpitations
- Stomach upset
- Sleep problems

Do you notice he shows signs of:

- Anxiety
- Restlessness
- Worrying
- Irritability
- Depression
- Sadness
- Anger
- Feeling insecure
- Lack of focus
- Burnout
- Forgetfulness

Does he exhibit these behaviors:

- Overeating
- Under eating
- Angry outbursts
- Drug or alcohol abuse
- Increased smoking
- Social withdrawal
- Crying spells
- Relationship conflicts

General Information

When a person has stress, it sets off the "fight or flight" response that goes back to caveman days. When confronted by a saber-toothed tiger, the caveman needed all his faculties to escape or fight the tiger. His body stops digestion and shoots adrenaline through his veins so that he has super-strength. His vision narrows, and hearing becomes acute.

Think for a moment how you feel when under severe stress – you are late for a very important meeting, and you cannot find your keys. Your heart pounds, your palms sweat, and you scan everywhere for those keys. You couldn't see them right there on the table where you looked because your vision has narrowed. Any sounds are either too loud or blocked out – you don't have the ability to focus on any additional information than that which will help you get to the meeting – even, or especially, a complaint from your child.

Now let's focus on your child. She is under acute stress all the time. She is trying so hard to achieve like a normal child, and act like a normal child, but is not complying. Any day at school is difficult. Social situations may be impossible; a birthday party may cause tears. Jessica actually thought she was retarded but was too afraid to let her mom know that anything was wrong. Instead she used her intelligence to "fake" being "normal".

The stress causes poor digestion. The food he/she is eating is not being fully digested, so he/she does not get the nutrients he/she needs. This causes him/her physical stress on top of his/her emotional stress, which comes back around, and causes more fight-or-flight response, which causes more poor digestion. You can see how tied together are the nutritional health and the mental health. Both should be worked on at the same time to break the cycle of stress and allow for the child to rest and repair.

There are many, many ways to combat stress. It can be done on your own, with help through technology, or with a professional. As with anything, a professional can probably help you get the results you want the quickest, but that option is usually the most expensive.

|Resources

Do It Yourself

• You can engage your child in deep breathing, physical activity, re-laxation techniques, meditation, or yoga at home to help with daily stress.

• Biofeedback: purchase Healing Rhythms from -
www.WildDivine.com.

• Various CDs that you could purchase that include meditations or calming music.

Professionals

• Consider a professional to help with biofeedback specifically designed for stress relief.

• Association for Applied Psychophysiology and Biofeedback go to:
www.aapb.org.

Chapter 4: Neurodevelopment: Primitive Reflexes

Success Story

I had lunch with the mother of a client I had worked with several months before. Ned had done his Primitive Reflex exercises for neurodevelopment simultaneously with listening therapy, followed by vision therapy and cognitive training. By the end of our working together, he had come so far and was much more able to read and write than before. Yet during lunch, the mom mentioned that his memory still wasn't where she would like it to be. I suggested that she have him do the primitive reflex exercises for Spinal Galant again to see if that opened up his memory. It only took two weeks to see a difference! It was as if a light bulb went off in his head, and he could now remember words from one page to the next.

Chelsea was a 12 year old girl who, probably because of brain surgery, had many difficulties learning math as well as other areas. She had retained the Moro reflex, so was doing her exercises for that stage of neurodevelopment every day. Her math difficulties were so strong that she was unable to correctly count the number of objects in any math example. There was no one-to-one correspondence. However, after a month of these 60 second exercises, her mother came to me to tell me the following story. Chelsea wanted a cassette at a store that was $7.99, and she had figured out that she had $5 at home, leaving $2.99, and her mother owed her $2 leaving $.99. She asked to borrow it, then her mother cried (from happiness) and gave her the $.99.

After 4 weeks of doing the exercises for the Tonic Labyrinthine Reflex, Maryanne told her mother that they had to hurry or they would be late to see Kathy (me) – up until this point, Maryanne didn't understand time at all, and 5 minutes had the same meaning as 30 minutes. Also, she was now able to describe in sequential detail how to do the swim strokes that she had learned over the weekend. By the time school started in the fall, she was in Middle School, and able to learn and retain information for the first time in her life.

Quiz

Mark which of the following symptoms are present, and score below:

Group #1 – The Moro Reflex
- Car sickness or poor balance and coordination
- Poor stamina
- Doesn't maintain eye contact
- Sensitive to light
- Sensitive to sound
- Allergies
- Adverse reaction to drugs
- Hypoglycemia
- Dislike of change
- Anxiety or nervousness
- Mood swings
- Poor math sense

Group #2 – Tonic Labyrinthine Reflex (TLR)
- Poor posture
- Weak muscles
- Poor balance
- Unable to cross eyes easily, or it hurts when crossing
- Spatial problems – bumps into furniture, stands too close
- Poor sequencing – telling stories, counting, organizing
- Poor sense of time, unable to tell time

Group #3 – Spinal Galant
- Fidgeting
- Bedwetting
- Poor concentration or attention
- Poor memory
- Very sensitive to several senses (visual, hearing, touch, smell,
- taste)
- Difficulty reading

Group #4 – Asymmetrical Tonic Neck Reflex (ATNR)
- Unable to cross eyes easily, or hurts when crossing
- Eyes jump over words or parts of words, or lines or repeats lines
- when reading
- Poor balance
- Right-left confusion
- Mixes up "d"s and "b"s or other letters and numbers
- Difficulty skipping or marching
- Poor handwriting
- Poor expression of ideas on paper

Group #5 – Symmetrical Tonic Neck Reflex (STNR)
- Poor posture
- Ape-like walk
- Poor eye-hand coordination
- Messy eater
- Unable to cross eyes easily, or hurts when crossing
- Slow with copying tasks
- Poor attention skills

Scoring

Number of Symptoms	Group and Reflexes
	Group 1 – Moro
	Group 2 – Tonic Labyrinthine Reflex (TLR)
	Group 3 – Spinal Galant
	Group 4 – Asymmetrical Tonic Neck Reflex (ATNR)
	Group 5 – Symmetrical Tonic Neck Reflex (STNR)

In reviewing the above list, if you saw a cluster of 3 or more symptoms, then there is reason to believe that some stages of neurodevelopment did not happen to a great enough degree, so read on for more about neurodevelopment.

General Information

When we are in utero and are infants, we go through stages of development that help us grow both physically as well as mentally. During these stages we naturally do certain physical movements that help us through each stage. We repeatedly do these movements, building muscle and opening pathways to our higher thinking brain, until we no longer need them. These stages are defined by the automatic reflexes, called primitive reflexes, that our bodies exhibit, that become inhibited once they are integrated.

A good example is the stage that includes the Tonic Labyrinthine Reflex (TLR). At this stage, from in utero to about 4 months, when placed on his tummy, a child will pick his head up, even though his head is about the same length and weight as the rest of his body. Where does he get the strength? He doesn't have it – it is a reflex that he cannot control. Meanwhile, while he continues to pick his head up, he gains control, builds muscle, and develops neurodevelopmentally. Some of the symptoms of a retained TLR are poor posture, inability to cross eyes, and poor sense of time.

There are five primitive reflexes that I work with, although this is just a subset of all. More information on this subject can be found in the book. Reflexes, Learning, and Behavior by Sally Goddard. The primitive reflexes that I work with cover the five groupings of symptoms found in the beginning of this chapter. The names, in order by group, are Moro Reflex, Tonic Labyrinthine Reflex (TLR), Spinal Galant, Asymmetrical Tonic Neck Reflex (ATNR), and Symmetrical Tonic Neck Reflex (STNR).

It takes just minutes a day to integrate these primitive reflexes at any age, beyond the early childhood stage. The exercises need to be done daily, or at least 5 times a week for about a month in order to see a change. I have seen children suddenly understand math, finally being able to memorize and remember, and for the first time being able to write a paragraph on their own.

One 10 year old boy, who had embarrassing bedwetting issues, had his first dry week after working on integrating the Spinal Galant.

These reflexes set up the body and mind to be able to work through the next phases in the Pyramid of Potential: the sensory-motor system, the cognitive development, and finally academics. If you are finding that issues are "stuck" then start here!!

Resources

Do It Yourself

• To learn more about the primitive reflexes, how to test for them, and how to remediate them, purchase The Pyramid of Potential Testing Module and the Pyramid of Potential DVD and Workbook Series. They go through all five levels of Primitive Reflexes plus other diagnostic tools and exercises to improve neurodevelopment. You can read more about this subject and purchase items at: www.PyramidOfPotential.com.

• Also available on the website is free information, links, and sign-ups for a free newsletter.

• DVD and information available at www.movetolearn.com.au

• DVD available from Sam Berne, OD at - www.newattention.net/dvds

• Trainings are available through:
  o www.MEDS-PDN.com – Dyslexia, Dyscalculia, and Dysgraphia course
  o RMT – www.rhythmicmovement.com
  o www.Masgutovamethod.com

• The best book on the subject is <u>Reflexes, Learning, and Behavior</u> by Sally Goddard.

Professionals

• In order to improve along the lines of these reflexes, the first step is to make sure that it is the reflex that causes the symptoms. Some Occupational Therapists (OT) help with this, so a call to the local OT in the yellow pages to find out if this is within their specialty is important. As of this writing, integrating the primitive reflexes is still fairly new in the USA.

• Check the web sites for RMT and Masgutova Method for local practitioners.

Chapter 5: Sensory-Motor Development: Sensory Integration

Success Story

When she was in 6th grade, Jessica and her mom went to see an Occupational Therapist, Judy, who gave the mom pages of paperwork to fill out and then tested Jessica in her OT room, filled with a swing, balls, and mats. The mom asked Judy if she was wasting time by coming, and she replied that no, Jessica was a classic case! The mom then wondered why no one had picked up on this when she was younger. I believe that teachers, especially primary level teachers, should be aware of what to look for in students, so that the children can receive services from the school OT if necessary.

Sensory Integration refers to the ability of the body to have an average sense of hearing, seeing, touching, smelling, and tasting, as well as balance and proprioception – the body's knowledge of itself in space using joints and muscles. For children who have sensory integration difficulties they are either hypersensitive (feel it excessively) or hyposensitive (barely feel it), and you will see many of the symptoms in the quiz below.

Quiz

- Picky eater (hypersensitive to taste)
- Eats EVERYTHING, including very spicy foods (hyposensitive to taste)
- Hates certain smells that are not offensive to others (hyper)
- Craves good smelling things – incense or candles (hypo)
- Hates to be touched (hyper)
- Craves hugs and touching soft blankets (hypo)
- Covers ears when in loud places (hyper)
- Always turns the radio louder (hypo)
- Cannot stand on one leg with eyes closed for more than 10 seconds (balance)
- Cracks knuckles, bumps into furniture, falls frequently (proprioception)

Sensory integration is probably an issue if 3 or more senses are off, or if you checked 3 or more of the symptoms above.

General Information

We can see an example of sensory integration dysfunction when a person either feels hypersensitive or hyposensitive to more than one or two of the senses at one time. For example, somebody who has hypersensitive hearing would hear better than most other people. He/she would not only be able to hear airplanes and cars approaching sooner than other people, but in a classroom he/she would also be able to hear the buzzing in florescent lighting, pencils scratching, chairs squeaking, birds chirping outside, the person walking down the hallway, and any whispering of the children as well as the teacher speaking. This cacophony makes it very difficult for him/her to be able to focus in on the teacher.

As you can imagine, this particular child might have the label of ADHD or ADD, because he is unable to focus when the teacher is speaking, when actually a more accurate diagnosis would be that of hypersensitive hearing.

Other children may be hypersensitive to bright lights when going from inside a building to the bright outdoors or when bright lights indoors bother them. Possibly even the bright white walls or sheets of paper that students are expected to read and work on bother them.

Another sense to which a child might be hypersensitive could be touch. This particular child would not like to be touched, would not like tags in his shirts, seams in his socks, tightness around his waistband, turtlenecks, long sleeves and jeans. This child would prefer comfy clothes.

Someone who is hypersensitive to the sense of taste would be considered a picky eater and probably would only like a few foods that are not particularly tasty or spicy.

Finally, a person who is hypersensitive to smells would not like normal smells and might find pleasant smells offensive: for example, bath or candle stores at the mall or even mom cooking hamburgers.

Alternatively, a child who is hyposensitive to these same things would be quite different. For example, a child who has hyposensitive hearing won't notice all those various sounds, wouldn't be bothered by loud sounds, and perhaps would even be recommended to have a hearing test done. He/she may not be able to distinguish between 'sh' and 'f', or between the vowel sounds. Yet, when tested, this child is said to have normal hearing.

A child who is hyposensitive to light would crave to see very bright colors and interesting objects with her eyes. A child who is hyposensitive to taste is very easy to spot because she eats things that no normal child would: jalapeño peppers and other spicy foods that are bursting with taste.

A child who is hyposensitive to smells would crave the smells of anything and enjoys smelling lotions and incense and possibly even gasoline. Children who are hyposensitive to touch would crave having people touch them and scratch their heads and rub their skin. They might rub their own skin.

There are two other senses beyond these two that I'd like to mention here. The first is the vestibular sense, which has to do with balance. The child whose vestibular sense is off probably has motion sickness and cannot read or do hand-held video games in the car. A child whose proprioceptive sense is off would be the child who can't get out of bed without stretching his/her legs and arms first. Also this child, when giving a hug, might want to give a very, very strong bear hug. This child alsoprobably cracks his/her knuckles.

When you see a child who exhibits many of these senses that are either hyper-sensitive or hyposensitive, that's when you see a child who probably has a sensory integration dysfunction.

You may wonder why this is even an issue for these children, and why does it matter to their success? These children feel uncomfortable all day long. They are not receiving correct information from their senses. The children may act cranky and irritable. In general, life is not very fun for this type of child.

In school, the problem becomes one where the child can't focus in on his class work. If his vestibular functioning is off, he is constantly adjusting himself because he's feeling out of balance. If he is hypersensitive to touch, he doesn't want to be near other people, and even his clothing bothers him.

If children are hypersensitive to sound, all the noise in the classroom is assaulting to their senses. If they're hypersensitive to smells, even smelling the lunch being cooked down in the cafeteria may distract them from doing their class work quickly and efficiently.

The hyposensitive children, because they are craving more sensory information, may be constantly touching other kids, asking repeatedly for the directions, looking everywhere instead of at the teacher, and may seem especially annoying to the other kids as they seek to fill the always empty sensory bucket.

By correcting these sensory issues, they will be able to function in the classroom much easier, and life in general will be much happier.

Resources

Do It Yourself

• The Out of Sync Child by Carol Stock Kranowitz.

• The Out of Sync Child Has Fun by Carol Stock Kranowitz.

Online

• Sensory Processing Disorder Foundation -
www.spdfoundation.net

• University of Southern California Occupational Therapy -
ot.usc.edu/academics/sensory-integration

Professionals

• See your yellow pages for occupational therapists who specialize in sensory integration dysfunction.

• www.spdfoundation.net for locating professionals in your area.

Chapter 6: Sensory- Motor Development: The Visual System, Vision Therapy and Irlen Syndrome

Success Stories

I want to tell a couple short stories here to explain how important the visual system is for overall functioning and for normal academic achievement.

The first one is about a young boy, Daniel, who was 12 years old and had been wearing glasses since he was four. He had been seeing optometrists basically all of his life. One day as I was speaking to him and looking in his eyes, one of his eyes took off and wandered around. It then came and joined the other as it looked at me. I said to him, "Do you see double vision?", and he replied "Yes, doesn't everyone?" That was the first time it really became clear to me that I had no idea what other people see. They also have no idea what we see, and we have no idea if what we are seeing is "normal". Ever since that day, I have never taken vision for granted.

The first year I worked with Chip on his reading, I noticed that he needed some vision help, so I sent him off to our local behavioral optometrist. At the same time, I was working with him on his reading. By the end of the year he was doing very, very well and had completely caught up.

The second year I worked with him, I noticed that he had back-tracked, and his vision was not where it should have been. He had a diagnosis of a fever syndrome that must have caused his body to lose developmental gains for the second year. Rather than asking the parents and the boy to go through vision therapy again, I decided to help him by integrating the primitive reflexes, an underlying cause of vision issues. Once again he did well, his vision improved and he was reading well. He had not lost the ability to read phonetically as I had taught him.

The third year when I went into work with him, his vision had once again regressed. I racked my brain for what I could do, since it was obvious that the exercises were not going to hold unless he did them every day for the rest of his life.

I had heard about Irlen syndrome and colored overlays (cellophane sheets). I purchased a set and screened him using this set to see if it made an improvement. Sure enough, when I put the green overlay on top of his book, he was surprised at how much better he could see.

From then on he used the green overlays rather than retraining his eyes. One of the most astounding stories I've ever heard was of Nathan, a young man who was put into a life skills class and told that he would never learn to read. He went to a behavioral optometrist and completed vision therapy, and with that alone, his reading level went up by years.

Once he could see better and his vision had improved, his mother advocated for him to get out of the life skills classroom and into mainstream classrooms. He was able to go into a college preparatory track in high school and has since graduated.

Quiz

These symptoms may indicate that you or your child has a vision problem.

- Red, sore or itching eyes
- Jerky eye movements, one eye turning in or out
- Squinting or excessive blinking
- Blurred or double vision
- Headaches, dizziness, or nausea after reading
- Head tilting, closing or blocking one eye when reading
- Avoidance of near work
- Frequent loss of place
- Omits, inserts, or changes letters or words
- Confuses similar looking words
- Failure to recognize the same word in the next sentence
- Poor reading comprehension
- Letter or word reversals after first grade
- Difficulty copying from the chalkboard
- Poor handwriting, misaligns numbers
- Book held too close to the eyes
- Inconsistent or poor sports performance

The above quiz came from PAVE: Parents Active for Vision Education.

More information can be found at www.pavevision.org.

General Information

When we think of vision, we usually think of acuity: being able to see clearly. But vision actually means much more than that. It encompasses not only what we see but how we process the information in our brains. For example, dyslexia is commonly referred to as a problem with mixing up the b's and d's and q's and p's. Also, a dyslexic may confuse the words saw and was. If this is the nature of the problem, then a more accurate diagnosis is a visual perception problem, which can be corrected through work on grounding, learning left from right, practicing visual discrimination, and training the brain.

Another vision issue that is commonly seen is the inability to track smoothly from left to right and from line to line. The child who cannot track well skips over words or parts of words, or might skip lines or repeat lines over and over again while reading. This lack of tracking ability makes it very difficult to have good comprehension while reading. Can you imagine how the comprehension of a person would be if they skipped over the word "not"? Tracking is a developmental issue and gets better with age, but once a person is beyond six or seven, he should be able to track quite smoothly.

Another vision issue is convergence, which refers to the ability to cross your eyes comfortably. When you're looking straight ahead and into the distance, your line of vision from both eyes is parallel, but as you focus in closer and closer to your nose, your eyes start to turn in. Some people have difficulty with this skill and find it uncomfortable to go from looking at a piece of paper on the desk to looking at a white board and then switching back again. It may take a second or two for their eyes to clear and become comfortable each time they go from the board to the paper.

Pediatrician's or kindergarten's visual screening usually includes the child standing 20 feet away from an eye chart and, with one eye covered, reciting the letters seen or the direction of E's. The reason for this test is of course to see how the child sees 20 feet away. If you think about the use in the classroom, you realize that this exercise is to help determine whether the child can see the whiteboard well.

This has nothing to do with how well the child can see reading a book. Some kindergarten screenings include testing for close vision, but most do not. You realize that it is up to the parent at some point to find out how good the child's acuity is.

On the website www.covd.org, it is recommended that children get a vision test every year and that they have their first vision test during toddlerhood. This way it can be determined early on whether there is an issue. The vision test should include not just an acuity test in order to see if they can see clearly, but it should also include testing for sustained focus, tracking, convergence, how well they can control their eyes' movement, and how well their eyes work together. The test should also include depth perception, form perception or how well they see and copy geometric figures, and visual memory. By including all of these things, it can be determined whether or not vision would be an issue with school work. If there are issues in these areas, there are a couple of methods that should be investigated to get relief.

Irlen Syndrome, or Scotopic Sensitivity Syndrome (SSS), has many of the same symptoms as visual dysfunction. By using colored overlays, many times these problems can be temporarily alleviated. You can learn more about this at www.Irlen.com. Where there are visual issues as described before, wearing colored lenses or using colored overlays can help the problems in a percentage of cases. A full set of colored overlays can be found in the Pyramid of Potential Test Module which can be purchased from www.pyramidofpotential.com.

The second thing that can be done to help out with visual problems is to see a behavioral or developmental optometrist. These specialists of optometry have had extra training beyond regular optometrists so that they can perform vision therapy. Typically, vision therapy includes an appointment in the office in addition to home exercises. In these exercises work is done on the vision system, both eyes and the brain to overcome issues that may be a problem. Although these issues may have started early in life, good vision can be developed at any time. The home exercises may last 15 minutes a day, and vision therapy may last anywhere from a couple of months to a year.

While working with my students I found that I needed many of these same trainings and therapies as well. One of the interventions that I completed was vision therapy. In the initial appointment while I was being tested, I had to look through something that looked like binoculars at a picture of an elephant. I started with my right hand and had to reach into a box and trace the element. No problem. Then I had to switch hands and trace the elephant with my left hand I found that when I looked throughthe binoculars I couldn't see my hand and the pencil. This particular device was able to show that I suppressed vision with my left eye when working on close projects. Vision therapy included, among other things, patching one eye at a time while reading as well as writing. Eventually my vision was much clearer, and I was able to read much faster and for longer periods of time.

A third way of correcting vision is through surgery by an ophthalmologist. I would caution anyone before having surgery done. One should explore all other noninvasive options before proceeding with surgery. In the book, Fixing My Gaze by Susan R. Barry, the author describes how she had surgery twice as a child because her eyes crossed. Despite the surgery, which made her eyes looked normal, they still did not work together. She assumed that she would never be able to have true depth perception. She went through vision therapy and describes how one day the steering wheel of her car popped right out. She had never seen in three dimensions before, and this was a startling and life changing discovery. Despite the widely held belief that "stereo vision", the ability to see in three dimensions, cannot be obtained past toddlerhood, Susan's experience shows that vision can be improved at any point in our lives.

Of all the trainings and therapies described in this book, vision therapy is perhaps the most profound and important. The methods described in previous chapters support vision and will help it develop faster and easier. The therapies in the following chapters all require good vision so that they can be done faster and easier. This should not be overlooked!

Resources

Do It Yourself

• Start with the Pyramid of Potential Test Module. In this module a screening is performed that includes tracking, convergence, peripheral vision, and an Irlen screening including colored filters of each of the colors. Go to www.PyramidOfPotential.com.

• Irlen overlays can be purchased individually at www.Irlen.com.

Online

• I have found no online resources for screening or remediating vision issues, however you may be able to purchase computerized software programs through a behavioral or developmental optometrist.

• www.COVD.org includes a plethora of information about vision.

Professionals

To find a professional, go to the following websites:
• www.covd.org

• www.visiontherapy.org

• www.irlen.com

Chapter 7: The Sensory Motor System: Auditory Development

Success Stories

Jason's mother said that the teacher had told her that her son could not hear the sound "r". He certainly spoke in such a manner that "r" was not frequently said. However, when I asked him which of the following two words was the thing like a toad, and then said fog and frog, he easily identified that the second word was the thing like a toad. So he could hear the "r" sound but perhaps did not process it well.

Allie had some significant auditory processing problems. Although she was not diagnosed specifically with Central Auditory Processing Disorder, she was hypersensitive to sounds, she could not pay attention to others when the TV was on, and she could not distinguish between the vowel sounds. I had her do some Listening Therapy, and at 11 years old she learned the vowels sounds and to read by sounding out words for the first time.

The following story is reproduced from Listening with the Whole Body, by Sheila M. Frick and Sally R. Young, with their permission. Charles (not his real name) was a 14-year-old eighth grader with a diagnosis of Autism Spectrum Disorder. Charles was referred by his mother due to concerns with poor social and motor skills. He struggled with listening in noisy environments, which made it difficult to understand the teacher and necessitated using closed-captioning while watching television. Prior to starting on the modulated Therapeutic Listening CDs, Charles's language was often hurried and mumbled. This made it difficult for him to make friends and he became very frustrated when people could not understand him.

After three months of Therapeutic Listening, Charles's perception of sound, particularly in complex auditory backgrounds, had improved dramatically. This, in turn, was reflected in his ability to articulate his own speech more clearly. One weekend at the museum, Charles's mother could clearly understand everything he said as he read the excerpts outside each exhibit. Since he was able to discriminate spoken words efficiently and effectively, he no longer needed to use the closed-captioning during television shows. He was now more confident in his ability to communicate with his peers and was able to make new connections.

On the Motor Coordination subtest of the Beery VMI, Charles made a gain of one year and one month in three months' time. His improvement in motor skills was reflected in his desire to participate in more athletic activities, whereas previously he was only interested in stationary activities such as drawing and watching television.

In June of 2006, Charles was screened for auditory processing difficulties using the SCAN-A, and the subtests for Filtered Words, Auditory Figure-Ground, Competing Words, and Competing Sentences were at the 5th percentile or lower, giving a Total Test Score in the 1st percentile (50th percentile is average). In August, after less than three months of Therapeutic Listening, the screening was again administered, and his Total Test Score was in the 87th percentile.

Quiz

- Hears extremely well or has hypersensitive hearing
- Talked late
- Mispronounces words
- Has difficulty with multi-step directions
- Has difficulty paying attention when the TV is on

General Information

Although the sense of hearing is just one of our many senses, it is one of the most important through which we receive our information daily. There are many reasons that someone's auditory systems may not work very well. One could be that auditory processing did not get well developed in infancy during neurodevelopment. Another reason could be through damage from ear infections, from exposure to loud noises, or environmental noises. Everyday noises with low tones such as motors cause damage in the inner ear. But sometimes this can be improved.

Central Auditory Processing Disorder (CAPD) is a diagnosis given if the person tested can hear appropriately but whose brain does not correctly process the sounds heard. They might be perceived as jumbled, too loud, or missing parts. The person might not be able to focus on the sounds when there are competing sounds in the room or in the other ear. You may have noticed this when speaking on the phone, if you have to plug your other ear in order to understand the person on the other end. You can hear him/her, but you cannot understand the words.

While working with my various students with auditory processing problems I recognized that I also have had issues along the same lines. Many times it takes me a second or two to interpret what I heard and make sense of it. I noticed it was really bad when my kids were small, sitting in the backseat of the car. I would hear, "Mom, mumble, mumble, mumble." I didn't know what they said! In order to understand what they were saying, I had to close the windows, turn off the radio and read their lips in the mirror.

Resources

Do It Yourself

• When Listening Comes Alive by Paul Madaule

Online

• Recently I have seen several new music programs available online and through your computer. These programs, listed below, are available to help increase auditory attention as well as to relax. In trying them myself, I've noticed that there has been a difference, and they are inexpensive enough to give it a try.

• www.mindstereo.com

• www.quantum-self.com Click on The Ultimate Brain Gym to see more information on Quantum Mind Power Gym.

Professionals

• Speech and language pathologists and occupational therapists specialize in this area.

• Therapeutic Listening can be found at - www.vitallinks.net.

• The Listening Program can be found at - www.thelisteningprogram.com.

• Samonas Listening can be found at www.samonas.com.

• More information about Auditory Integrated Therapy can be found at www.aitinstitute.org.

• More information about Tomatis can be found at - www.tomatis.com

Chapter 8: Sensory Motor Development: Motor Development

Success Story

Once I was working with a young boy, Evan, who was about 10 years old. I was working with him on cognitive training, which is an intensive program of one hour a day, six days a week. He was progressing okay, but after only about 3 weeks he was unable to progress.

Some of the activities that I give the children to wake up their brain while we are working are to drink water, to take a walk, or to do a "lazy eight" which is a Brain Gym® activity that forces the children to cross the midline of their body. I noticed that Evan could not do the lazy eight well. So I taught him how, using a piece of paper and having him trace this large figure. By doing this several times it forces the left and right hemispheres of his brain to work together in a more coordinated fashion. This activity gives his brain more access to both hemispheres at the same time.

Although the day that I started training him on this activity he did not progress very much, I had him take this exercise home and do it every day for homework. Approximately 2 weeks later he was able to do a lazy eight in the air on his own, and the day he could do that, he progressed miles ahead of the days before. His brain had taken a cognitive leap, and the progress was due to being able to cross the midline.

Quiz

- Does the child have difficulty with the following:
- March using opposite arm and leg, skip, or swim the crawl
- Stand on 1 leg with eyes closed for 10 seconds
- Clap to a beat
- Hit, throw, or kick a ball
- Handwriting

General Information

It may not seem obvious at first that motor activities have anything to do with academics, but consider this: in order to have good handwriting, you must have good fine motor control. In order to have good fine motor control, you must have good gross motor control. In order to have good gross motor control, you must have gone through your primitive reflexes, especially the second, third, and fourth levels that were described in Chapter 4.

Crossing the Midline

In order to access your full brain to do complicated tasks such as handwriting, you need to be able to access both sides of the brain at the same time. The left side of your brain contains the language center, while the right side is used for creative endeavors, like creating sentences. Since the left side of your brain is attached to the right side of your body and the right side of your brain is attached to the left side of your body, the best way to activate both sides of your brain is to move both sides of your body at the same time. One way to be able to do this is to cross the midline.

The midline is the invisible line through the middle of your body from your head to your toes. To cross the midline, you would move your left arm or leg to the right side of your body, or visa-versa. Another thing you could do is move one arm at the same time as the opposite leg, as in marching or skipping. This forces both sides of your brain to work at the same time.

Balance

The vestibular system, which includes the sense of balance, is one of the first to be created in the womb and is the basis for the earliest development of the entire mind-body system. It is the basis of organization for the other senses to develop, creates our sense of three dimensional space, and is the foundation for our perceptions.
The sense of balance is created during several of the primitive reflexes, so therefore it should be worked on in conjunction with primitive reflex training. See Chapter 4.

A good sense of balance comes from good inner ears, which are related to good hearing and good listening. Good hearing and good listening are required for good academics. Also poor balance would make it difficult to sit still in a chair. This student would be very fidgety and unable to concentrate on what the teacher is saying.

To sum up the importance of a good sense of balance, it is an important building block to brain development and organization. If you know of a child who is disorganized, you probably will find that this child has a poor sense of balance.

Timing

The ability to keep a beat is developed in the frontal lobe. The frontal lobe is where the executive manager part of the brain resides and is that which helps us control our attention and behavior.

Keeping a beat is also associated with the ability to tell time. It is an important element in communication, especially verbal communication. Good verbal communication requires good timing.

The inability to keep the beat has been associated with autism and with ADD/ADHD.

Many professionals, such as physical therapists, occupational therapists, educators, speech and language pathologists, and behavioral and developmental optometrists, are available to help with motor development.

Resources

Do It Yourself

• "Movement is the door to learning" was said by Paul Dennison, the creator of Brain Gym®. Brain Gym® is an entire program that was originally created by Edu-Kinesthetics to help people who have had traumatic brain injury. It is now used for neurodevelopment for all types of individuals. It's a simple exercise program that helps develop the brain and make connections between all parts of the brain. More can be learned, and resources can be purchased, at www.braingym.com. It is used by occupational therapists all over the world. A wonderful book is the Teacher's Manual, which includes many of their exercises.

• Bal-A-Vis-X is an inexpensive program that was created tom increase balance so children's brains work better. It includes many activities and several instruments. More can be learned about this at www.bal-a-vis-x.com.

• www.learningbreakthrough.com has a kit which includes balance and sensory integration activities.

• Go to www.metronomeonline.com for... you guessed it – a free metronome on the internet. You can use it any time you are online, and it works very well!

Professionals

• One of the best ways to get better at keeping a beat is the use of a metronome, and an entire program was built around this.
Astounding results have been found through the use of Interactive Metronome. More information and providers can be found at - www.interactivemetronome.com.

• Look in the Yellow Pages for Occupational Therapists, Speech and Language Pathologists, and Physical Therapists.

Chapter 9: Cognitive Development

Success Story

When Bill was just nine years old, his parents brought him to me to work with him. We did three months of a cognitive training program which yielded the result that his scores improved by over 13 years total. The comments that his parents made afterwards were "he has shown a significant improvement in his ability to do his schoolwork. Before using this program, he would continually moan and groan over everything! ... It is such a joy to see his face light up because he finally gets it! When we started, his math average was on the verge of an F. As we near the final marking period, he has brought it up to a B!! I noticed his attitude overall has changed. He is more willing and with less complaining, helps around the house. He plays Little League baseball, and this is the first year I have not had to remind him about good sportsmanship."

I received a call from an unexpected source – a 70 year old woman, Alice, who had had a stroke. She wondered if I could help her with her word retrieval. Although I had never worked with anyone like this before, I am always willing to try. When we first began she told me how difficult it was to retrieve words in a general conversation, causing her to describe the thing or action instead of naming it. Her frustration was high.

We used the BrainSpark! program and I worked with her one hour a day, three days a week. Alice did an hour of homework between sessions. Early on, I asked her to tell me the direction of some arrows on a card. There were 4 arrows across, and 6 arrows down the page. Her choices were up, down, left, or right. She knew the directions with no problem, so all she had to do was to retrieve four different words. The first row was to be "up, left, left, left". She said: "Um, up. Um, left. Um, um, um..." She was unable to retrieve the word "left" that she had just one second before said. I was hoping I could help her.

We struggled through that page, then changed directions to give her a break and did some motor exercises to a metronome. We went back to the page using the metronome at a slow pace. We went back and forth between the page of arrows and the motor exercise, increasing the rate of the metronome each time. Finally, we quit when she reached 120 beats per minute, saying the direction every other beat.

We then moved on to other exercises, working to the beat, increasing the number of items for her to retrieve. At the end of 10 weeks, she was happy to finish the cognitive training, while able to spend an hour on the telephone with a friend while only one word retrieval problem. Her goal was accomplished!

Quiz

- Does not read up to grade level
- Has poor math skills
- Difficulties with math word problems
- Poor comprehension
- Poor memory
- Slow in completing work
- Poor attention
- Poor spelling
- Poor writing skills
- Avoids schoolwork
- Works too hard on schoolwork
- Reversals of letters, numbers or words
- Loses place and skips lines
- Poorer motivation or behavior
- Low self-esteem

General Information

It used to be thought that IQ could not change. Today, psychologists know that the brain can and does change. This is great news for people with academic struggles! Now it is a matter of determining where the deficit lies and then strengthening the brain in that area.

There are many cognitive training programs available today. I have used a few of them. I have found PACE to be very effective, but it is not available in all areas of the country or the world, and requires a trained provider. I have also used BrainSpark!, an at-home kit with as much success.

As you evaluate programs to see which would be the most effective, be sure that they include many different cognitive skills, and not just one or two.

Also note that many of the cognitive training programs include sections that help with visual and auditory processing. In order to get the most out of a cognitive training program, it is best to lay the groundwork through the bottom of the Pyramid of Potential. This way, the neurodevelopment has happened, the senses are modulated, motor abilities are developed, and then cognitive abilities can be targeted. Any cognitive strengthening program will work better if the groundwork is laid down first.

Also, in order to maximize the results plan on high intensity as well as high frequency of training. It should be completed daily and never be too easy. The brain needs to be stimulated in order to change. However, it must also be motivating. If the training is too difficult motivation will decrease. It is a rare person who will be so self-motivated that they would work hard with no visible gains or accomplishments!

Connections in the brain are made by creating a new neural pathway between cells and then strengthening that pathway through repeated use. That is why it takes 21 days to create a new habit. Think of cognitive skills as many different new habits or ways of thinking.

Here are some of the important skills that should be included in a cognitive training program, as described by PACE.

• Processing speed is the ability to do easy cognitive tasks quickly.

• Working memory is the ability to remember and retrieve information. Also, it refers to the working space in memory used to manipulate information.

• Visual processing is the ability to use pictures in our mind and manipulate them, such as in geometry or jigsaw puzzles.

• Auditory analysis is the pre-reading skills, including blending sounds together (for reading), segmenting sounds (for spelling), and sound manipulation (say frog without the 'f').

• Logic/reasoning skills are used for higher conceptual thinking and deductive reasoning used for math word problems and understanding similes and metaphors. Concrete thinkers are usually lacking in age appropriate logic and reasoning skills.

• Selective visual attention is the ability to pay attention to one visual input (the teacher) when there are many competing inputs (word wall, bulletin boards, other kids). It is difficult for people with poor selective visual attention to work on math sheets with 20 or 30 problems to a page.

PACE, BrainSpark! and other cognitive training programs work on additional areas such as auditory-visual association, comprehension, divided attention, long-term memory, as well as short-term memory, math computations, saccadic fixation (movement of the eyes quickly from one point to another), sensory motor integration, sequential processing as well as simultaneous processing, sustained attention, visual discrimination, visualization and visual span.

The benefits of training with a cognitive program go beyond just the abilities to help with academic struggles. Sure, they help with reading, spelling, math, word problems and reading comprehension, but they also are good for problem solving, listening comprehension, completing tasks quickly, sports, card games, jigsaw puzzles and remembering names.

Resources

Do It Yourself

• Brain Spark! can be purchased through www.pyramidofpotential. com. This is a comprehensive cognitive training program that can be done at home. I have worked with students using Brain Spark! and found it to be extremely thorough, user friendly, good for a large variety of ages, and especially good for those with vision and attention issues.

• Another program that can be used at home is Audiblox. Although I have not used it, I have heard that it is quite good. See www. audiblox2000.com.

Online

• You can do a cognitive screening of your child through the Gibson's test at www.pyramidofpotential.com. This will give you a list of skills and a beginning point to find out how your child is doing as you complete various trainings and therapies.

• The Brain Skills core exercise program is an online program to increase cognitive skills, found at www.brainskills.com.

• The Brainware Safari program is an online cognitive training program suitable for young children. More information can be found at www.brainwareforyou.com.

Professionals

• To find a PACE provider in your area go to -
www.processingskills.com

• To find providers for Audiblox go to -
http://www.audiblox.com/WorldMapSelect

• Learning Rx Centers were created by the developers of PACE and exist in many states in the US. You can find more information and locations at: www.learningrx.com.

Chapter 10: Academic Intervention

Success Story

Once I had decided to tutor reading, I needed a good program. I considered getting trained in several different intensive, but expensive programs. Then a friend told me of a book that I should try, so I bought Reading Reflex by Carmen and Geoffrey Mc Guinness. I read it over the weekend and started the program with my first student, Jessica, the next Monday. We spent one hour a day for the next 20 school days, and at the end she was reading above grade level. I'll never forget when she was reading a gum wrapper after that and said, "I never could have read this before!" I thought I had found the silver bullet.

I worked with Allan on reading every school day for a year. When we started, he was in 6th grade but was 14 years old due to being retained twice. I told him he would read 100 books this year and they could be any books he chose. He returned from the bookcase with The Little Engine That Could, a picture book. I learned that day that Allan was a nonreader, that retention did not help him read, and that passing him along did not help him read. So, I taught him to read.

The first thing I did was to teach him the pre-reading skills of blending sounds together into a word, pulling sounds out of a word (segmenting), and finally manipulating sounds in words. I then taught him the 44 sounds in our language along with how they are spelled, as is taught in Reading Reflex. Finally we worked on syllables until he could decode grade appropriate text. He could read!

However, after reading a paragraph, when I asked him what happened, he said he didn't know. I realized that he truly did not know what he just read. When we would first start talking each day, I would ask him questions about what he did over the weekend or what he had for dinner the night before. He would say he didn't know. I thought he was being a typical teenage boy. Through this close work with him I realized that he had no visualizations in his head to draw on, and therefore his memory was weak.

Not all people have a movie going on in their head while reading stories, but many do, and this is how they comprehend and store the information. I knew I needed to teach Allen how to visualize. By using Visualization and Verbalization by Lindamood-Bell within weeks he was able to visualize objects, then actions, and finally a series of actions from reading paragraphs. He learned to summarize and finally was no longer a nonreader.

Jennifer struggled in math. In fourth grade she could remember the facts but not easily understand the concepts. I used a math program called Math-U-See to tutor her. By working one-on-one, she was allowed to go at her own pace. I started with basic concepts, and used her strongest mode of learning – visualizing – to help her get to grade level. By completing four lessons a week, she was able to learn about two years worth of math in just seven months.

My biggest lesson? There is no silver bullet for success as every person learns differently, and there are no shortcuts. The brain is a complicated tool that permeates our entire being; in order to solve one simple problem we must truly look at the whole person.

Quiz

Is your child underachieving academically, whether it is reading, writing, math or other subjects?

General Information

Reading

Teaching reading has gone through many different variations over the last couple years. Years ago only phonics was taught. Then there was a rush through the United States to teach everybody using whole language. These two methods are quite different in that phonics teaches decoding of words through word families and letter combinations. Whole language, on the other hand, teaches reading real books and the memorization of whole words.

The majority of children can learn to read, no matter what the method. They use their deductive reasoning powers, memory and knowledge of the English language to figure out what reading is all about. Unfortunately there are a large number of people who struggle, where something is missing. They may not process the English language well. Or they may not process the sounds of the spoken word well. Or they may not get the meanings of the words as they are put together. Something else is needed.

Phonemic awareness is the term used to describe being aware of the sounds in a word, being able to manipulate them, separate them and put them back together. Blending is putting sounds together to make word. For example, if you put the sounds "c" "a" "t" together you get the word cat. Segmenting is taking the sounds apart and this is done whenever a word is being spelled. For example, if you were to segment the word frog, you would come out with the sounds "f" "r" "o" "g". Notice that I did not blends the sounds "f" and "r" together. In order to spell well, it's important to be able to segment down to the individual sound level.

Another skill that is very important in the ability to read is learning the skill of manipulating sounds within a word, for example being able to easily say desk without the "d". This of course would give you "esk". The hardest is to easily say desk without the "s" to give you "dek". For some children that has to be studied and practiced numerous times in order for it to become automatic.

Why do they need this? So that while they are sounding out a word they are listening for the real word. They need to be able to play with sounds in their mind quickly and easily to be able to come up with the correct words. If they get bogged down in decoding, they lose comprehension due to forgetting the words that they had previously read.

The very best book that I ever read on learning and teaching reading is a book by Diane McGuinness called Why Our Children Can't Read. It challenged me to listen to the words and the sounds that I speak and to really think about how they are taught.

Several new reading programs have come out of McGuinness's method of teaching sounds rather than letters. The basic premise is that there are only 44 sounds in the English language and that we have heard sounds since before we were born. This means that naturally we are going to learn to read easier if we start at the sound level rather than at the letter. One of the reasons phonics may not work as well for some children who struggle with reading is that it works on letter combinations, of which there are 1500. There is a lot less data to learn and understand if only working with the 44 sounds.

When deciding how to proceed with what program to use to remediate reading, please make sure that you have followed the Pyramid of Potential and that both the processing of hearing and sight are at optimal levels and cognitive processing has been improved in most areas. Cognitive processing programs usually include phonemic awareness so that the prereading skills of blending, segmenting and auditory analysis have already been remediated. So at this point, all that needs to be done is learning the code. By the code, I mean learning that the letter combination of "oa" in the word "boat" will have the "long o" sound, or that "kn" sounds like "n".

Math

What can cause math problems for a child? For a child who has good vision, it could be number sense, it could be memory. It could be logic and reasoning.

For a child who has poor number sense, it's possible that the neurodevelopment never happened. That would open up the brainstem pathways to the higher parts of the brain. For more information, read the chapter on neurodevelopment in Chapter 4.If you are sure that the neurodevelopment has happened, there are some programs that teach about number sense and understanding mathematics, not just memorizing facts. These are listed in the resource section at the end of this chapter.

Does the child have a good memory? Can the child recall the facts quickly and easily? If not, a good cognitive training program is in order.

When Anne was young, she had difficulty in math because she had a small active working memory. She could only keep a few pieces of information in memory at a time. In her younger elementary school years, she was able to memorize her math facts fairly easily, and she understood the math concepts well. Her problem was that she was unable to put these things together at the same time in her mind. Her digit span was extremely small, meaning that she could only keep about 2 to 3 pieces of information in her mind at a time. In fourth grade the class started to do double digit multiplication, but this was beyond her capabilities.

Until she completed a cognitive training program, she was unable to progress without aids, such as a calculator. Once she completed PACE, a cognitive training program, she was able to do math easily and quickly, and her math teacher exclaimed that it was a miracle!

For a child who has been left behind in math it is difficult to catch up in later years. A good foundation is so important to being able to understand and learn the more complicated math concepts. I suggest that you use one of the programs listed in the resource section after remediating any cognitive challenges. Go back to the basics and build from there. This may take extra time and seem redundant at times, but filling in the gaps will reap great rewards.

Writing

The act of writing is the most difficult academic process we have that we demand of our students. It starts with being able to hold the writing instrument well, remembering how to form each letter, remembering how to spell a word or at least sounding out a word, remembering and forming a sentence that is being created, remembering and creating the paragraph that's being worked on, and finally keeping the organization of the entire piece in mind.

If your child has difficulty writing, start at the base of the Pyramid of Potential. Be sure that there is little stress being put on that child, either through foods he might be allergic to or through psychological stress. It does not help to make the child feel that writing is this huge, important academic necessity.

Make sure that the neurodevelopment has happened to open up the pathways to the brain to make writing easier. The fourth level of neurodevelopment - the primitive reflex of ATNR - is very important to complete in order to write well. See chapter 4.

Continuing up the Pyramid of Potential, large motor and fine motor development needs to be completed. The child should have plenty of muscle development in his hands, arms, shoulders, back and neck in order to be able to easily perform the physical act of writing.

In the cognitive level, a sufficient active working memory is very important in order to write well. There must be enough room to remember how to form the letters, spelling, mechanics, and the concepts. Also at this level good logic and reasoning skills are important. In order to write complex concepts, good logical understanding is required.

Finally, once all of the underlying skills are in place, any good writing program that directly and explicitly teaches writing should be sufficient.

Other academic subjects

It is my belief that once the underlying skills plus the previously mentioned academic subjects have been remediated, a student should be sufficiently successful in the other academic subjects.

Resources

Do It Yourself

Reading

• Why Our Children Can't Read by Diane McGuinness

• Reading Reflex by Carmen and Geoffrey McGuinness

• How to Increase Your Child's Verbal Intelligence by Carmen McGuinness

• Sound Reading Solutions Program by Bruce Howlett – www.soundreading.com

• ABeCeDarian Reading Program by Michael Bend – www.abcdrp.com

• Visualization and Verbalization by Lindamood-Bell

Math

• Math U See Program by Steven Demme – www.mathusee.com

• Math Makes Sense! Program - www.soundreading.com/Mathinstruction. html

Professionals

Reading

• Master The Code from PACE providers –
www.ProcessingSkills.com

• Phonographix Providers -
www.readamerica.net/searchallmembers.asp

Other Learning Centers for Reading, Writing, and Math

• Sylvan – www.sylvan.learning-centers.com

• Huntington – www.huntingtonlearning.com

• Learning Rx – www.learningrx.com

Chapter 11: Putting It All Together

General Information

You may have skipped around this book and looked for information that pertains to your unique situation. I hope that you found information that was relevant and informative and ultimately useful.

Do it yourself, on-line, or use professionals? It is a matter of time, quality, and money. Doing it yourself may be less expensive, but in general it is less effective. This can be for several reasons. I found it harder to work with my own children than it is to work with strangers who are too polite to argue with me. Also, the more I work with my clients, the more experience I have, and the better quality service I give. I know that I can, as a professional, get faster and better results than someone who has not worked as long as I have with these tools and these children.

If you are willing to work with your child, and your child is willing to work with you, try doing it yourself first. Usually the initial investment is not too large. If the first try is not successful, try hiring a tutor to use the program you choose or you can go to a professional.

Perhaps you want to try on-line help where available. It is generally less expensive and more convenient than using a professional. More experience is behind the
creation of an on-line program, so you might be able to expect better results than doing it yourself. The biggest problem here is motivation. It takes a large amount of motivation to do a difficult task repeatedly when a warm, encouraging teacher is not there to make it easier. When I am working with a child, I am careful to watch the emotions he or she is exhibiting in order to determine my next tasks. This is of course lost when working with a computer, unless you or a tutor sits with him or her.

You are ultimately the one who decides the process and the provider of any trainings and therapies to help your child. Carefully consider all aspects, look for guarantees and testimonials, and speak to others who have used this service before. Each step should result in a progressive and positive step toward success, not frustration and discouragement.

Before I understood the power of the Pyramid of Potential, sometimes I would work with the child at a higher level than he needed. For example, I might do a cognitive training program before having the child complete vision therapy. There have been times when I have interrupted the cognitive training, sent the child off to do vision therapy, and then finished cognitive training much more successfully and easily following the vision therapy.

I have also mistakenly thought that any child had the ability to be successful at cognitive training. Then I found that it was easier and faster to complete the cognitive training if I had him do the neuro-development first. The same was true with trying to teach reading to a child who needed cognitive training or vision therapy. I found that we could only progress so far without the underlying skills being remediated first. When working with parents to decide the process of helping their child, we usually go through two scenarios. The first scenario is the fast way. Here, we may start with nutrition, neurodevelopment, listening therapy and possibly even vision therapy, all at the same time. Then, three months later, we start the cognitive training. In this way most of the remediation is complete within six months.

The problem with this scenario is that the remediation, though quick, is rarely as thorough as it would be if each therapy was completed one at a time. For older kids in middle school and high school, the summer is the best time to complete remediation and therapies. The school year is so filled with homework and sports that there is not enough time to concentrate on these therapies. Therefore, sometimes the quick method is the only way. Cognitive training for one hour every day can only be considered in the summer for older children.

The younger child has more time before the demands of school are as rigorous as they are in middle and high school. If time is not of the essence, if the child is younger, or if you are home-schooling, a slow but steady progression through the Pyramid of Potential is recommended.

Start with nutrition and dietary changes. If there is any anxiety, use whatever methods you deem best to reduce that anxiety. Follow this with a 5 to 6 month series of neurodevelopment to open up the pathways to the higher cognitive parts of the brain that will set up for all other processes to work.

The next step is to work on sensory motor development. A thorough assessment by an occupational therapist versed in sensory integration is a good choice. It is very important to have a thorough assessment by a behavioral or developmental optometrist to determine whether vision therapy or glasses are necessary. The remediation at this level can take a full three to six months or more.

Once all of these physical skills are solid, it is time to move on to cognitive training. The amounts of gains that can be made are much greater in the cognitive areas if the foundation is laid. A solid three-month cognitive training program, done for one hour almost every day, will reap amazing benefits.

After completing all of these levels, which may take more than a year, academic remediation should be quick and easy. Now that the child can learn, it is a matter of filling in the gaps and bringing him up to grade level.

Good luck on your journey with all of the children you help along the way. I hope someday that your success story will be inspiration for others as well.

References

Bell, N. (1991) Visualizing and Verbalizing. Gander Educational Publishing, San Luis Obispo, CA

Berne, S. A. (2005) Creating Your Personal Vision. Color Stone Press, Santa Fe, NM

Berne, S. A., (2002) Without Ritalin. Keats Publishing/McGraw Hill, New York

Eden, D. (2004) The Energy Medicine Kit. Sounds True, Boulder, CO

Freed, J., Parsons, L., (1997) Right-Brained Children in a Left-Brained World. Simon & Schuster, New York

Frick, S. M., Young, S. R., (2009) Listening with the Whole Body. Vital Links, Madison, WI

Gibson, K. (2007) Unlocking the Einstein Inside. Learning Rx, Colorado Springs, CO

Goddard, S., (2002) Reflexes, Learning and Behavior. Fern Ridge Press, Eugene, OR

Gold, S. J. (1997) If Kids Just Came With Instruction Sheets! Fern Ridge Press, Eugene, OR

Hallowell, E. M., Ratey, J. J., (2006) Delivered From Distraction. Ballantine Books, New York

Hannaford, C., (1995) Smart Moves. Great Ocean Publishers, Alexander, NC

Hannaford, C., (1997) The Dominance Factor. Great Ocean Publishers, Alexander, NC

Hyman, M. (2009) <u>The UltraMind Solution.</u> Scribner, New York

Irlen, H. (2005) <u>Reading by the Colors.</u> Penguin Group, New York

Kranowitz, C. S. (1998) <u>The Out-of-Sync Child.</u> Perigee Books, New York

Kranowitz, C. S. (2003) <u>The Out-of-Sync Child Has Fun.</u> Perigee Books, New York

Larsen, S. (2006) <u>The Healing Power of Neurofeedback.</u> Healing Arts Press, Rochester, VT

Levine, M., (1994) <u>Educational Care. Educators Publishing Service, Inc.,</u> Cambridge, MA

Madaule, P. (1994) <u>When Listening Comes Alive.</u> Moulin Publishing, Norval, Ontario

McGuinness, C., McGuinness, G. (2000) <u>How to Increase Your Child's Verbal Intelligence.</u> Yale University Press, New Haven

McGuinness, D. (1997) <u>Why Our Children Can't Read.</u> The Free Press, New York

Pauc, R. (2007) <u>The Brain Food Plan.</u> Virgin Books Ltd, London

Remick, K. M., Stroud, C. A., Bedes, V., (2000) <u>Eyes On Track.</u> JF's Publishing, Folsom, CA

Vitale, B. M., (1982) <u>Unicorns are Real.</u> Warner Books, New York

Wilkins, A. (2003) <u>Reading Through Colour.</u> John Wiley & Sons, Ltd, West Sussex, England